Whales

James Maclaine

Illustrated by Sara Ugolotti

Designed by Sam Whibley, Tom Lalonde and Nelupa Hussain

Whale consultant: Professor Steve Simpson, Marine Biology and Global Change, University of Bristol

Contents

Ocean giants

Whales are very big animals that live in seas and oceans around the world. There are lots of different types.

This is a blue whale.

Blue whales are the biggest animals that have ever lived.

How whales swim

Whales swim slowly for very long distances. They can also be surprisingly fast.

These whales are called orcas.

They flick their strong tails up and down to push through the water.

To change direction, whales move two parts called flippers.

Some whales swim in groups known as pods.

Whales sometimes swim on their backs.

Coming up for air

Whales breathe air through holes on top of their heads. They're called blowholes.

When a pilot whale needs air, it swims to the surface.

First, it breathes out from its blowhole, making a misty spray.

Then its blowhole gets wider as it breathes in fresh air.

Its blowhole closes before it goes back below the water.

This is a pod of four humpback whales.

They have swum up together to breathe.

Some types of whales have a pair of blowholes.

Great big mouths

Some whales have teeth. Others have stiff, bristly combs called baleen instead.

See how the baleen hangs from the top of this young whale's mouth.

Whales use their baleen when eating.

First, a bowhead whale fills its mouth with thousands of little creatures called krill.

Then it closes its mouth. The baleen catches the krill but lets water out.

Orcas use their teeth to bite the animals they eat.

Above water

Sometimes, whales can be seen above the surface of seas and oceans.

This humpback whale is leaping up into the air.

It's called breaching.

Whales breach to make a big splash and show off.

Some whales play in waves made by boats.

Spyhopping is when whales bob up to look around.

These orcas can stay like this for a few minutes.

Rubbing clean

Whales need to keep their skin clean.

Every summer, tiny plants grow on beluga whales' skin.

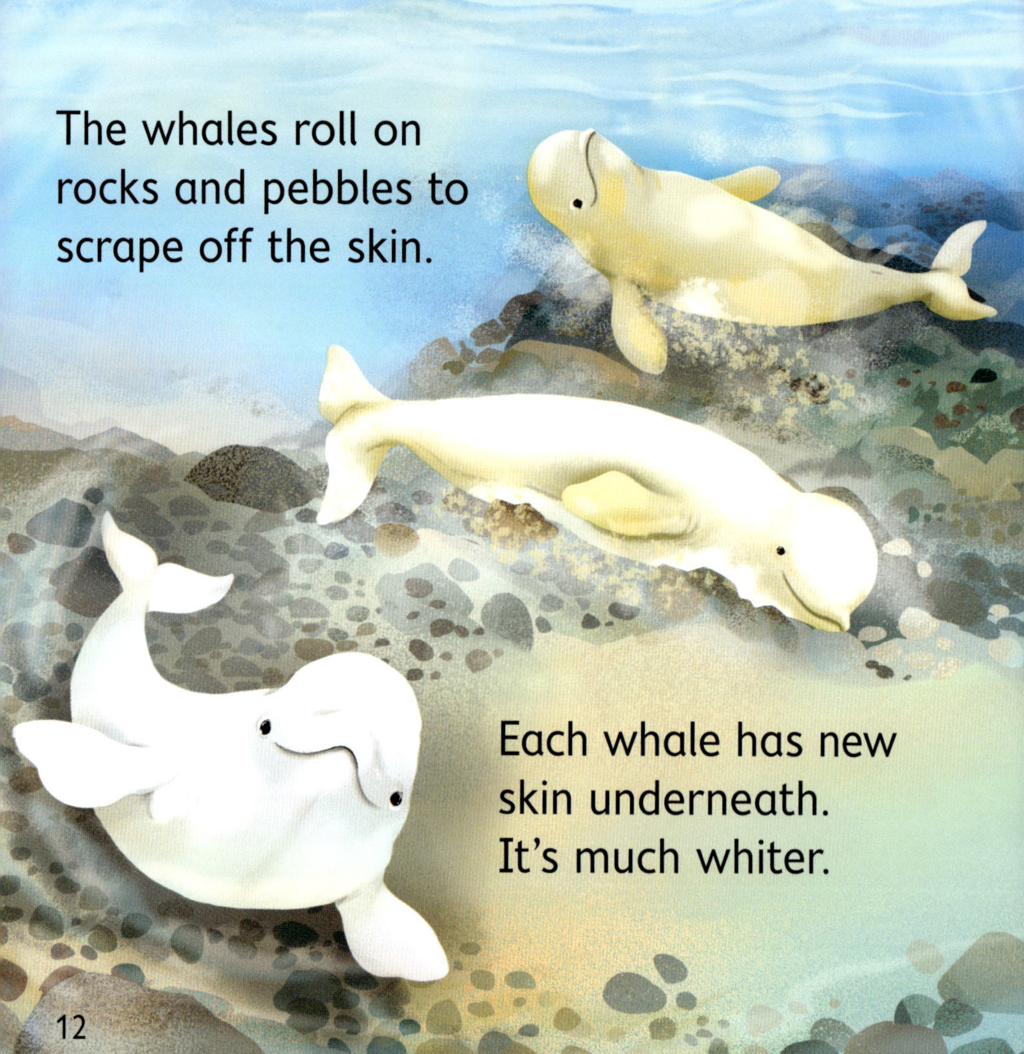

The whales roll on rocks and pebbles to scrape off the skin.

Each whale has new skin underneath. It's much whiter.

These sperm whales are rubbing against one another. This makes their old skin peel away.

Thank you!

Fish called remoras eat tiny creatures that cling to whales' skin.

Mother whales

Mother whales carry their babies inside them for up to a year and a half.

A mother humpback whale swims a long way to find warm, shallow water.

Here, it's safe for her baby to be born. It comes out tailfirst. It's called a calf.

The calf needs air. Its mother nudges it up to the surface so it can breathe.

This beluga whale calf is leaning on its mother.

The calf's skin starts to turn white as it gets older.

Many baby whales are born with little whiskers on their faces.

Growing up

It takes many months for whale calves to grow up.

This sperm whale calf is drinking milk from its mother's body.

The milk is very fatty. It helps the calf get bigger fast.

Whale calves try to stay very close to their mothers.

It's less tiring for this calf to swim at its mother's side.

Mother orcas teach their calves how to hunt.

Nice catch!

Noisy whales

Whales make lots of different sounds to talk to other whales.

Whales from the same pod whistle to each other as they swim.

A mother whale and her calf whisper softly to help them stay together.

Male humpbacks sing the same songs again and again. No one knows why they do it.

Whales slam their tails on the surface...

...to show other whales where they are.

Scientists use underwater microphones to listen to whales.

Expert hunters

Orcas use all sorts of tricks to catch animals to eat.

Some orcas leap out of the sea to chase after dolphins.

Some slap stingrays with their tails to stop them moving.

Other orcas charge at floating ice to knock seals into the water.

Orcas even hunt other kinds of whales.

This orca is lunging onto the seashore...

...to try to snatch a sea lion.

Deep-sea divers

Some whales dive down very deep to search for things to eat.

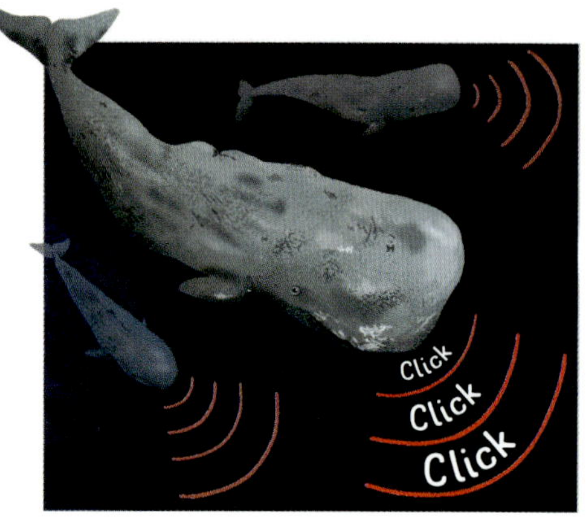

It's dark in the deep sea. Sperm whales make clicking sounds to help find their way.

When the whale's clicks hit a squid, they bounce back to the whale.

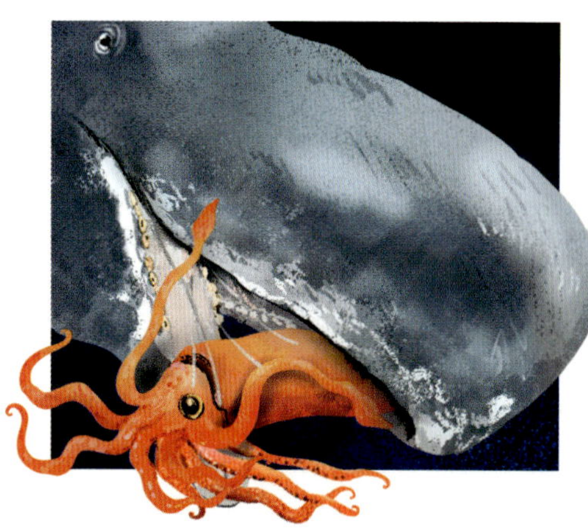

Now the whale knows where to strike. It sucks the squid into its mouth.

These pilot whales stay underwater for about fifteen minutes when they dive.

Beaked whales dive the deepest. Their dives can last for an hour.

Blowing bubbles

Whales can blow out air underwater. Some humpback whales do this to trap fish with bubbles.

1. One whale swims in circles, blowing rings of bubbles for a net.

2. Down below, other whales chase fish into the bubbles.

3. Suddenly, one of the whales makes a loud noise.

4. This tells the other whales to zoom up, through the bubbles.

5. Then they open their mouths wide to eat the fish.

Whales also blow bubbles when they're playing.

Very long teeth

Narwhals live in the icy waters of the Arctic Ocean.

This male narwhal has a long, spiral-shaped tooth. It's called a tusk.

A few males have two tusks. Female narwhals don't have any.

Narwhal tusks are very useful.

Longer tusks make male narwhals look more impressive to females.

Narwhals hit fish with their tusks to stop them moving. Then they eat the fish.

Young narwhals sometimes rub their tusks together to say hello.

Time to rest

Whales take lots of short naps each day.

Orcas stay still, just below the surface of the water. They wake up to breathe.

When a humpback whale calf feels tired, it lies on top of its mother.

This sleepy sperm whale is resting in an upright position.

Only sperm whales are known to sleep like this.

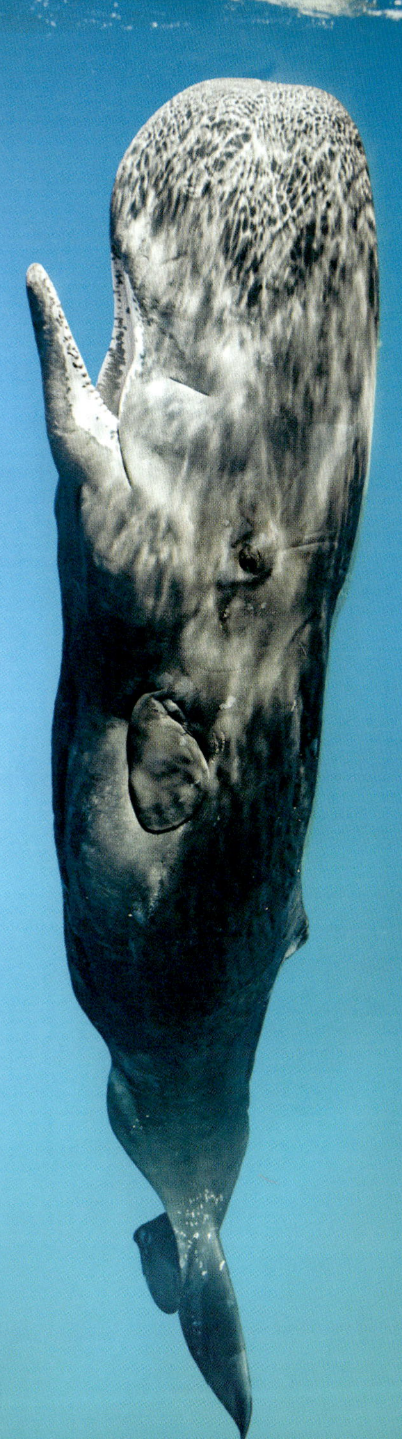

Beluga whales keep one eye open while they rest.

Glossary

Here are some of the words in this book you might not know. This page tells you what they mean.

flipper – a flat body part used for swimming. Whales have two flippers.

pod – a group of whales. Many types of whales live in pods.

blowhole – a hole on a whale's head. It opens when a whale breathes.

baleen – fine, stiff combs in some whales' mouths. Baleen traps food.

krill – little shrimps that live in the sea. Some whales eat lots of krill.

calf – a baby whale. Mother whales have one calf at a time.

tusk – a long tooth. Tusks stick out from some whales' mouths.

Usborne Quicklinks

Would you like to find out even more about whales? Visit Usborne Quicklinks for links to websites with videos, facts and activities.

Scan the code or go to **usborne.com/Quicklinks** and type in the keywords "**beginners whales**". Make sure you ask a grown-up before going online.

Notes for grown-ups

Please read the internet safety guidelines at Usborne Quicklinks with your child. Children should be supervised online. The websites are regularly reviewed and the links at Usborne Quicklinks are updated. Usborne Publishing is not responsible for the content or availability of external websites.

People go whale watching on boats. If they're lucky, they might see a whale dive.

Index

Acknowledgements

Additional illustrations by Gal Weizman
Photographic manipulation by John Russell
Series designer: Helen Edmonds

Photo credits

The publishers are grateful to the following for permission to reproduce material:
cover © All Canada Photos / Alamy Stock Photo; **p.1** © D. Parer & E. Parer-Cook / Minden / naturepl.com; **pp.2-3** © Blue Planet Archive / Phillip Colla; **pp.4-5** © Serge MELESAN / 500px / Getty Images; **p.7** © Juan Maria Coy Vergara / Getty Images; **p.8** © Chase Dekker / Minden / naturepl.com; **p.10** © Blue Planet Archive / Jon Cornforth; **p.11** © Espen Bergersen / naturepl.com; **p.13** © Media Drum World / Alamy Stock Photo; **p.15** © Blue Planet Archive / imageBROKER / Andrey Nekrasov; **p.16** © Media Drum World / Alamy Stock Photo; **p.17** © Mark Carwardine / naturepl.com; **p.19** © Matthew Maran / naturepl.com; **p.21** © Sylvain Cordier / naturepl.com; **p.23** © Doug Perrine / naturepl.com; **p.26** © Blue Planet Archive / Ursus / John K. B. Ford; **p.29** © Jordi Chias / naturepl.com; **p.31** © Norbert Wu / Minden / naturepl.com.

First published in 2025 by Usborne Publishing Limited, 83-85 Saffron Hill, London EC1N 8RT, United Kingdom. usborne.com UE. First published in America 2025.